FOREST'S ROBE

PENHALIGON'S SCENTED TREASURY
OF AUTUMN VERSE AND PROSE

To Cousin Louise

FOREST'S ROBE

EDITED BY
SHEILA PICKLES

LONDON MCMXCII

INTRODUCTION

Dear Reader,

When I began to think about which pieces I might include in this anthology on the season of autumn, I was concerned that my task would be arduous. I have tended to think of autumn simply as the transition time between summer and winter and assumed that others thought likewise. Therefore I was happily surprised to discover that as a season it inspires passionate feelings and divided opinions among great writers and artists. For Laura in *Lark Rise to Candleford*, it was the culmination of the hamlet year, when the whole village played its part in bringing in the harvest and celebrated with the harvest festival.

I found that autumn is particularly welcomed·in the country. With the glorious changing shades of the trees, harvesting of crops and gathering of produce from the hedgerows for jams and jelly-making, it is a time of fulfilment both for the farmer and the housewife.

In the city, however, the autumn brings wet pavements and the foggy weather so evocatively captured in *Bleak House* by Charles Dickens. Then, just when the season seems at its most dismal, the excitement of halloween and bonfire night brings delight to child and adult alike. Pagan fires, lanterns and jewel-like explosions into the frosty dark, these are the joys of autumn to Robert Louis Stevenson.

The joys are many, and I hope this selection will re-awaken in you an appreciation of this season of rich colours and change, as it has in me.

Sheila Pickles, Yorkshire, 1992

POT-POURRI

When autumn winds blow and leaves fall from the trees, the forest floor becomes a valuable source of material for pot-pourri. Walking through the woods, I always make for the river bank where the fir trees thrive. There fir cones, pine cones, nuts and seed pods may all be gathered up and dried and made into a decorative mix with a seasonal feel. I collect anything with a pretty colour and shape, even skeleton leaves, which will add interest to my bowl or basket.

Bark from trees absorbs scent well, but of course must never be picked off the trunk as it damages the tree. Small twigs and windblown branches can be taken home and the bark removed when dry.

Hedge clippings from box or privet may be made into a bunch and hung upside down to dry, the small leaves adding colour and variety. It is always better to dry greenery over an air flow and an airing cupboard with wooden slats is ideal.

In the autumn, when the hydrangeas change colour, they should be cut before they are full out, hung upside down and dried. In this way, they will retain their glorious colour all year round and may be used whole, or their petals broken up for smaller arrangements.

When all the components have been dried they may be mixed together in a large bowl. Pot-pourri will have an autumnal scent of its own but a few drops of essential oil may be added, according to taste.

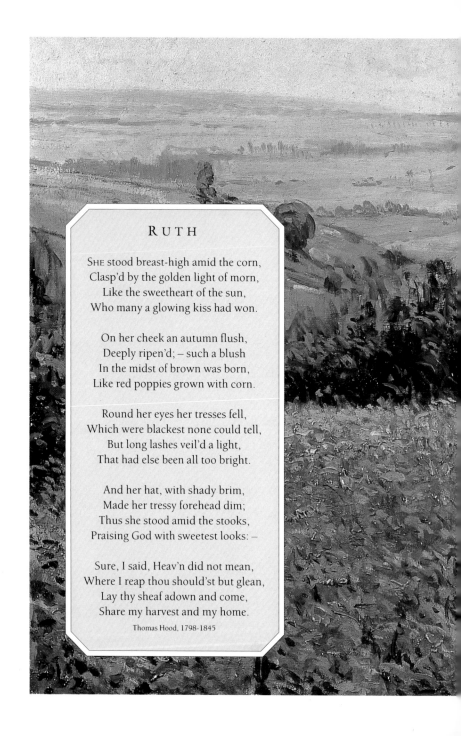

RUTH

SHE stood breast-high amid the corn,
Clasp'd by the golden light of morn,
  Like the sweetheart of the sun,
Who many a glowing kiss had won.

On her cheek an autumn flush,
Deeply ripen'd; – such a blush
  In the midst of brown was born,
Like red poppies grown with corn.

Round her eyes her tresses fell,
Which were blackest none could tell,
  But long lashes veil'd a light,
That had else been all too bright.

And her hat, with shady brim,
Made her tressy forehead dim;
  Thus she stood amid the stooks,
Praising God with sweetest looks: –

Sure, I said, Heav'n did not mean,
Where I reap thou should'st but glean,
  Lay thy sheaf adown and come,
Share my harvest and my home.

Thomas Hood, 1798-1845

AUTUMN

AUTUMN in felted slipper shuffles on,
Muted yet fiery, — Autumn's character.
Brown as a monk yet flaring as a whore,
And in the distance blue as Raphael's robe
Tender around the Virgin.
Blue the smoke
Drifting across brown woods; but in the garden
Maples are garish, and surprising leaves
Make sudden fires with sudden crests of flame
Where the sun hits them; in the deep-cut leaf
Of peony, like a mediaeval axe
Of rusty iron; fervour of azalea
Whose dying days repeat her June of flower;
In Sargent's cherry, upright as a torch
Till ravelled sideways by the wind to stream
Disorderly, and strew the mint of sparks
In coins of pointed metal, cooling down;
And that true child of Fall, whose morbid fruit
Ripens, with walnuts, only in November,
The Medlar lying brown across the thatch;
Rough elbows of rough branches, russet fruit
So blet it's worth no more than sleepy pear,
But in its motley pink and yellow leaf
A harlequin that some may overlook
Nor ever think to break and set within
A vase of bronze against a wall of oak,
With Red-hot Poker, Autumn's final torch.

Vita Sackville-West, 1892-1962

TUSCAN THOUGHTS

ONE evening, when he had gone out thus, Lilia could stand it no longer. It was September, Sawston would be just filling up after the summer holidays. People would be running in and out of each other's houses all along the road. There were bicycle gymkhanas, and on the 30th Mrs Herriton would be holding the annual bazaar in her garden for the C.M.S. It seemed impossible that such a free, happy life could exist. She walked out onto the loggia. Moonlight and stars in a soft purple sky. The walls of Monteriano should be glorious on such a night as this. But the house faced away from them.

Perfetta was banging in the kitchen, and the stairs down led past the kitchen door. But the stairs up to the attic – the stairs no one ever used – opened out of the living-room, and by unlocking the door at the top one might slip out onto the square terrace above the house, and thus for ten minutes walk in freedom and peace.

The key was in the pocket of Gino's best suit – the English check – which he never wore. The stairs creaked and the keyhole screamed; but Perfetta was growing deaf. The walls were beautiful, but as they faced west they were in shadow. To see the light upon them she must walk round the town a little, till they were caught by the beams of the rising moon. She looked anxiously at the house, and started.

It was easy walking, for a little path ran all outside the ramparts. The few people she met wished her a civil good-night, taking her, in her hatless condition, for a peasant. The walls trended round towards the moon; and presently she came into its light, and saw all the rough towers turn into pillars of silver and black, and the ramparts into cliffs of pearl. She had no great sense of beauty, but she was sentimental, and she began to cry; for here, where a great cypress interrupted the monotony of the girdle of olives, she had sat with Gino one afternoon in March, her head upon his shoulder, while Caroline was looking at the view and sketching.

From *Where Angels Fear to Tread* by E. M. Forster, 1879-1970

A MELLOW AFTERNOON

Thursday, 24 September, 1874

THIS afternoon I walked over to Kington St. Michael by Langley Burrell Church and Morrell Lane and the old Mausoleum and Langley Ridge and the Plough Inn. It was a day of exceeding and almost unmatched beauty, one of those perfectly lovely afternoons that we seldom get but in September or October. A warm delicious calm and sweet peace brooded breathless over the mellow sunny autumn afternoon and the happy stillness was broken only by the voices of children blackberry gathering in an adjoining meadow and the sweet solitary singing of a robin.

As I drew near Kington I fell in with a team of red oxen, harnessed, coming home from plough with chains rattling and the old ploughman riding the fore ox, reminding me vividly of the time when I used to ride the oxen home from plough at Lanhill.

In spite of the warm afternoon sunshine the solitary cottages, low lying on the brook, looked cold and damp, but the apples hung bright on the trees in the cottage gardens and a Virginia creeper burned like fire in crimson upon the wall, crimson among the green. When I returned home at night the good Vicar accompanied me as far as the Plough Inn. The moon was at the full. The night was sweet and quiet. Overhead was the vast fleecy sky in which the noon was riding silently and the stillness was broken only by the occasional pattering of an acorn or a chestnut through the leaves to the ground.

From *The Diary of the Reverend Francis Kilvert*, 1840-1879

ENDYMION

So, she was gently glad to see him laid
Under her favourite bower's quiet shade,
On her own couch, new made of flower leaves,
Dried carefully on the cooler side of sheaves
When last the sun his autumn tresses shook,
And the tann'd harvesters rich armfuls took.
Soon was he quieted to slumbrous rest:
But, ere it crept upon him, he had prest
Peona's busy hand against his lips,
And still, a-sleeping, held her finger-tips
In tender pressure. And as a willow keeps
A patient watch over the stream that creeps
Windingly by it, so the quiet maid
Held her in peace: so that a whispering blade
Of grass, a wailful gnat, a bee bustling
Down in the blue-bells, or a wren light rustling
Among sere leaves and twigs, might all be heard.

O magic sleep! O comfortable bird,
That broodest o'er the troubled sea of the mind
Till it is hush'd and smooth! O unconfin'd
Restraint! imprisoned liberty! great key
To golden palaces, strange minstrelsy,
Fountains grotesque, new trees, bespangled caves,
Echoing grottoes, full of tumbling waves
And moonlight; aye, to all the mazy world
Of silvery enchantment! – who, upfurl'd
Beneath thy drowsy wing a triple hour,
But renovates and lives? – Thus, in the bower,
Endymion was calm'd to life again.

John Keats, 1795-1821

A U T U M N A L

Pale amber sunlight falls across
The reddening October trees,
That hardly sway before a breeze
As soft as summer: summer's loss
Seems little, dear! on days like these

Let misty autumn be our part!
The twilight of the year is sweet;
Where shadow and the darkness meet
Our love, a twilight of the heart
Eludes a little time's deceit.

Are we not better and at home
In dreamful Autumn, we who deem
No harvest joy is worth a dream?
A little while and night shall come,
A little while, then, let us dream.

Beyond the pearled horizons lie
Winter and night; awaiting these
We garner this poor hour of ease,
Until love turn from us and die
Beneath the drear November trees.

Ernest Dawson, 1867-1900

THE HAYLOFT

THROUGH all the pleasant meadow-side
The grass grew shoulder-high,
Till the shining scythes went far and wide
And cut it down to dry.

These green and sweetly smelling crops
They led in waggons home;
And they piled them here in mountain tops
For mountaineers to roam.

Here is Mount Clear, Mount Rusty-Nail,
Mount Eagle and Mount High; –
The mice that in these mountains dwell,
No happier are than I!

O what a joy to clamber there,
O what a place for play,
With the sweet, the dim, the dusty air,
The happy hills of hay.

Robert Louis Stevenson, 1850-1894

Apple-Picking

THERE were a great many holidays at Plumfield, and one of the
most delightful was the yearly apple-picking – for then the
Marches, Laurences, Brookes, and Bhaers turned out in full force,
and made a day of it. Five years after Jo's wedding one of these
fruitful festivals occurred. A mellow October day, when the air
was full of an exhilarating freshness which made the spirits rise,
and the blood dance healthy in the veins. The old orchard wore its
holiday attire; golden-rod and asters fringed the mossy walls;
grasshoppers skipped briskly in the sere grass, and crickets
chirped like fairy pipers at a feast. Squirrels were busy with their
small harvesting, birds twittered their adieux from the alders in
the lane, and every tree stood ready to send down its shower of red
or yellow apples at the first shake. Everybody was there –
everybody laughed and sang, climbed up and tumbled down;
everybody declared that there never had been such a perfect day
or such a jolly set to enjoy it – and everyone gave himself up to the
simple pleasures of the hour as freely as if there were no such
things as care or sorrow in the world.

Mr March strolled placidly about, quoting Tusser, Cowley, and
Columella to Mr Laurence, while enjoying

'The gentle apple's winy juice'.

The Professor charged up and down the green aisles like a stout
Teutonic knight, with a pole for a lance, leading on the boys who
made a hook-and-ladder company of themselves, and performed
wonders in the way of ground and lofty tumbling. Laurie devoted
himself to the little ones, rode his small daughter in a bushel
basket, took Daisy up among the birds' nests, and kept adventur-
ous Rob from breaking his neck. Mrs March and Meg sat among the
apple piles like a pair of Pomonas, sorting the contributions that
kept pouring in; while Amy, with a beautiful motherly expression in her face, sketched the various groups, and watched over
one pale lad who sat adoring her with his little crutch beside him.

From *Good Wives* by Louisa M. Alcott, 1832-1888

THE WIND

I SAW you toss the kites on high
And blow the birds about the sky;
And all around I heard you pass,
Like ladies' skirts across the grass –
O wind, a-blowing all day long,
O wind, that sings so loud a song!

I saw the different things you did,
But always you yourself you hid.
I felt you push, I heard you call,
I could not see yourself at all –
O wind, a-blowing all day long,
O wind, that sings so loud a song!

O you that are so strong and cold,
O blower, are you young or old?
Are you a beast of field and tree,
Or just a stronger child than me?
O wind, a-blowing all day long,
O wind, that sings so loud a song!

Robert Louis Stevenson, 1850-1894

THE PLOUGH

ABOVE yon sombre swell of land
Thou see'st the dawn's grave orange hue,
With one pale streak like yellow sand,
And over that a vein of blue.

The air is cold above the woods;
All silent is the earth and sky,
Except with his own lonely moods
The blackbird holds a colloquy.

Over the broad hill creeps a beam,
Like hope that gilds a good man's brow;
And now ascends the nostril-stream
Of stalwart horses come to plough.

Ye rigid Ploughmen, bear in mind
Your labour is for future hours:
Advance – spare not – nor look behind –
Plough deep and straight with all your powers!

Richard Henry Horne, 1803-1884

— 23 —

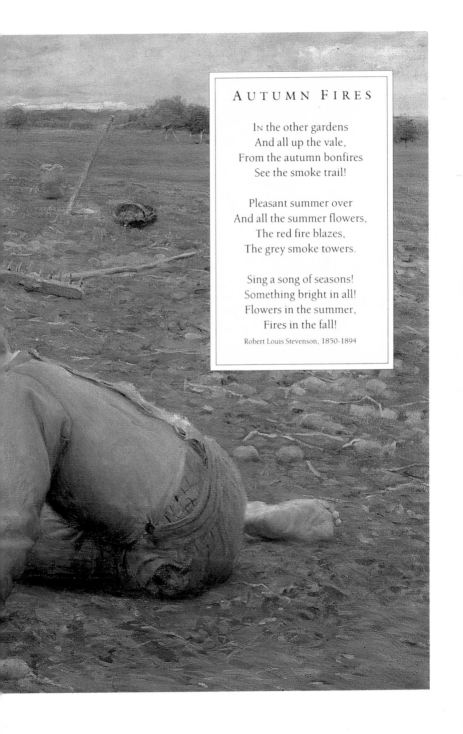

AUTUMN FIRES

In the other gardens
And all up the vale,
From the autumn bonfires
See the smoke trail!

Pleasant summer over
And all the summer flowers,
The red fire blazes,
The grey smoke towers.

Sing a song of seasons!
Something bright in all!
Flowers in the summer,
Fires in the fall!

Robert Louis Stevenson, 1850-1894

MICHAELMAS EVE

MICHAELMAS-EVE happening on the next day, we were invited to burn nuts and play tricks at neighbour Flamborough's. Our late mortifications had humbled us a little, or it is probable we might have rejected such an invitation with contempt; however, we suffered ourselves to be happy. Our honest neighbour's goose and dumplings were fine, and the lamb's wool, even in the opinion of my wife, who was a connoisseur, was excellent. It is true his manner of telling stories was not quite so well; they were very long and very dull, and all about himself, and we had laughed at them ten times before; however, we were kind enough to laugh at them once more.

Mr Burchell, who was of the party, was always fond of seeing some innocent amusement going forward, and set the boys and girls to blind-man's buff. My wife, too, was persuaded to join in the diversion, and it gave me pleasure to think she was not yet too old. In the meantime, my neighbour and I looked on, laughed at every feat, and praised our own dexterity when we were young. Hot cockles succeeded next, questions and commands followed that, and, last of all, they sat down to hunt the slipper. As every person may not be acquainted with this primeval pastime, it may be necessary to observe that the company at this play planted themselves in a ring upon the ground, all except one, who stands in the middle, whose business it is to catch a shoe which the company shove about under their hams from one to another, something like a weaver's shuttle. As it is impossible in this case for the lady who is up to face all the company at once, the great beauty of the play lies in hitting her a thump with the heel of the shoe on that side least capable of making a defence. It was in this manner that my eldest daughter was hemmed in and thumped about, all blowzed in spirits, and bawling for fair play, with a voice that might deafen a ballad-singer, when, confusion on confusion, who should enter the room but our two great acquaintances from town, Lady Blarney and Miss Carolina Wilhelmina Amelia Skeggs!

From *The Vicar of Wakefield* by Oliver Goldsmith, 1730?-1774

HARVEST TIME

Iɴ the fields where the harvest had begun all was bustle and activity. At that time the mechanical reaper with long, red, revolving arms like windmill sails had already appeared in the locality; but it was looked upon by the men as an auxiliary, a farmers' toy; the scythe still did most of the work and they did not dream it would ever be superseded. So while the red sails revolved in one field and the youth on the driver's seat of the machine called cheerily to his horses and women followed behind to bind the corn into sheaves, in the next field a band of men would be whetting their scythes and mowing by hand as their fathers had done before them.

With no idea that they were at the end of a long tradition, they still kept up the old country custom of choosing as their leader the tallest and most highly skilled man amongst them, who was then called 'King of the Mowers'. For several harvests in the 'eighties they were led by the man known as Boamer. He had served in the Army and was still a fine, well-set-up young fellow with flashing white teeth and a skin darkened by fiercer than English suns.

With a wreath of poppies and green bindweed trails around his wide, rush-plaited hat, he led the band down the swathes as they mowed and decreed when and for how long they should halt for 'a breather' and what drinks should be had from the yellow stone jar they kept under the hedge in a shady corner of the field. They did not rest often or long; for every morning they set themselves to accomplish an amount of work in the day that they knew would tax all their powers till long after sunset. 'Set yourself more than you can do and you'll do it' was one of their maxims, and some of their feats in the harvest field astonished themselves as well as the onlooker.

From *Lark Rise to Candleford* by Flora Thompson, 1876-1947

WILD PLUM JAM

To some people autumn is a time of fulfilment, to others it is when one makes preparations for the next year's flowers and fruits, and I suppose the autumn of life can be much the same if we can only really believe all we are told. I for one cannot, so I live on from day to day, doing whatever turns up to do, and hoping for the best even if I do not think it will ever come. At any rate, it is a mercy to have done with mental strife, to feel agony, sheer, searing agony, soften into dulled pain; to even enjoy the beautiful weather and to be amused at Marjorie, at the blackberry forays, and the pickling and preserving that go on in the kitchen, because the maids are delighted to be able to make real jam and no longer depend on the 'bought stuff' on which we have existed in London without any qualms at all. Once more one sees the horrible waste that goes on in the country, and notices how little is made of the bountiful provision given free gratis and for nothing by Nature herself. I know hedges in Buckinghamshire, for example, where the crab-apples, wild plums and blackberries are just snatched at, half ripe, by passing children, but which are wholly neglected by those who could an they would make jam, jelly and cordial to keep the household going all through the year.

From *Leaves from a Garden* by Miss S. E. Parton, 1910

— 30 —

INDIAN SUMMER

O CTOBER 15. – This is St. Luke's summer, or the 'Indian summer' as it is called in America. The air is soft and warm and still. The yellow leaves fall from the Beeches in countless numbers, but slowly and noiselessly, and as if reluctant to let go their hold. The rooks come back to us again across the fields, and clamour among the empty nests, which were their homes in spring. The 'remontant' Roses are putting out their latest blooms, and the Antirrhinums, Mulleins, and some other flowers, show themselves 'remontant' also. There is an aromatic fragrance everywhere from the withering leaves and from the lingering flowers.

But there is sadness with it all. We cannot deceive ourselves, but we know that all is now over, and that at any moment the frost may come, and leave us nothing but decay and death.

From *A Year in a Lancashire Garden* by Henry A. Bright, 1891

AUTUMN STARS

WHEN they came in they sat beside the fire in the oak drawing-room, and Darrow noticed how delicately her head stood out against the sombre panelling, and mused on the enjoyment there would always be in the mere fact of watching her hands as they moved about among the tea-things . . .

They dined late, and facing her across the table, with its low lights and flowers, he felt an extraordinary pleasure in seeing her again in evening dress, and in letting his eyes dwell on the proud shy set of her head, the way her dark hair clasped it, and the girlish thinness of her neck above the slight swell of the breast. His imagination was struck by the quality of reticence in her beauty. She suggested a fine portrait kept down to a few tones, or a Greek vase on which the play of light is the only pattern.

After dinner they went out on the terrace for a look at the moon-misted park. Through the crepuscular whiteness the trees hung in blotted masses. Below the terrace, the garden drew its dark diagrams between statues that stood like muffled conspirators on the edge of the shadow. Farther off, the meadows unrolled a silver-shot tissue to the mantling of mist above the river; and the autumn stars trembled overhead like their own reflections seen in the water.

From *The Reef* by Edith Wharton, 1862-1937

THROUGH THE WOODS

OTHER memories of those early years remained with her as little pictures, without background, and unrelated to anything which went before or came after. One was of walking over frosty fields with her father, her small knitted-gloved hand reaching up to his big knitted-gloved hand and the stubble beneath their feet clinking with little icicles until they came to a pinewood and crept under a rail and walked on deep, soft earth beneath tall, dark trees.

The wood was so dark and silent at first that it was almost frightening; but, soon, they heard the sounds of axes and saws at work and came out into a clearing where men were felling trees. They had built themselves a little house of pine branches and before it a fire was burning. The air was full of the sharp, piny scent of the smoke which drifted across the clearing in blue whorls and lay in sheets about the boughs of the unfelled trees beyond. Laura and her father sat on a tree-trunk before the fire and drank hot tea, which was poured for them from a tin can. Then her father filled the sack he had brought with logs and Laura's little basket was piled with shiny brown pine-cones and they went home. They must have gone home, although no trace of memory remained of the backward journey: only the joy of drinking hot tea so far from a house and the loveliness of shooting flames and blue smoke against blue-green pine boughs survived.

From *Lark Rise to Candleford* by Flora Thompson, 1876-1947

SONNET

That time of year thou may'st in me behold
When yellow leaves, or none, or few, do hang
Upon those boughs which shake against the cold –
Bare ruin'd choirs where late the sweet birds sang.
In me thou see'st the twilight of such day
As after Sunset fadeth in the West,
Which by and by black night doth take away,
Death's second self, that seals up all in rest.
In me thou see'st the glowing of such fire
That on the ashes of his youth doth lie,
As the death-bed whereon it must expire,
Consumed with that which it was nourish'd by.
This thou perceiv'st, which makes thy love more strong
To love that well which thou must leave ere long.

William Shakespeare, 1564-1616

An Ominous Visit

O N the following morning Mrs Dale and Bell were sitting together, Lily was above in her own room, either writing to her lover, or reading his letter, or thinking of him, or working for him. In some way she was employed on his behalf, and with this object she was alone. It was now the middle of October, and the fire was lit in Mrs Dale's drawing-room. The window which opened upon the lawn was closed, the heavy curtains had been put back in their places, and it had been acknowledged as an unwelcome fact that the last of the summer was over. This was always a sorrow to Mrs Dale; but it is one of those sorrows which hardly admit of open expression.

'Bell,' she said, looking up suddenly; 'there's your uncle at the window. Let him in.' For now, since the putting up of the curtains, the window had been bolted as well as closed. So Bell got up, and opened a passage for the squire's entrance. It was not often that he came down in this way, and when he did so it was generally for some purpose which had been expressed before.

'What! fires already?' said he. 'I never have fires at the other house in the morning till the first of November. I like to see a spark in the grate after dinner.'

'I like a fire when I'm cold,' said Mrs Dale. But this was a subject on which the squire and his sister-in-law had differed before, and as Mr Dale had some business in hand, he did not now choose to waste his energy in supporting his own views on the question of fires.

'Bell, my dear,' said he, 'I want to speak to your mother for a minute or two on a matter of business. You wouldn't mind leaving us for a little while, would you?' Whereupon Bell collected up her work and went upstairs to her sister. 'Uncle Christopher is below with mamma,' said she, 'talking about business. I suppose it is something to do with your marriage.' But Bell was wrong. The squire's visit had no reference to Lily's marriage.

From *The Small House at Allington* by Anthony Trollope, 1815-1882

O CTOBER

O HUSHED October morning mild,
Thy leaves have ripened to the fall;
Tomorrow's wind, if it be wild,
Should waste them all.
The crows above the forest call;
Tomorrow they may form and go.
O hushed October morning mild,
Begin the hours of this day slow.
Make the day seem to us less brief.
Hearts not averse to being beguiled,
Beguile us in the way you know.
Release one leaf at break of day;
At noon release another leaf;
One from our trees, one far away,
Retard the sun with gentle mist;
Enchant the land with amethyst.
Slow, slow!
For the grapes' sake, if they were all,
Whose leaves already are burnt with frost,
Whose clustered fruit must else be lost –
For the grapes' sake along the wall.

Robert Frost, 1874-1963

DESOLATE

THE Day goes down red darkling,
The moaning waves dash out the light,
And there is not a star of hope sparkling
On the threshold of my night.

Wild winds of Autumn go wailing
Up the valley and over the hill,
Like yearning Ghosts round the world sailing,
In search of the old love still.

A fathomless sea is rolling
O'er the wreck of the bravest bark;
And my pain-muffled heart is tolling,
Its dumb-peal down in the dark.

The waves of a mighty sorrow
Have whelmèd the pearl of my life:
And there cometh to me no morrow
Shall solace this desolate strife.

Gone are the last faint flashes,
Set is the sun of my years;
And over a few poor ashes
I sit in my darkness and tears.

Gerald Massey, 1828-1907

BAVARIAN GENTIANS

NOT every man has gentians in his house
in Soft September, at slow, Sad Michaelmas.

Bavarian gentians, big and dark, only dark
darkening the day-time torch-like with the smoking blueness of Pluto's gloom,
ribbed and torch-like, with their blaze of darkness spread blue
down flattening into points, flattened under the sweep of white day
torch-flower of the blue-smoking darkness, Pluto's dark-blue daze,
black lamps from the halls of Dis, burning dark blue,
giving off darkness, blue darkness, as Demeter's pale lamps give off light,
lead me then, lead me the way.

Reach me a gentian, give me a torch
let me guide myself with the blue, forked torch of this flower
down the darker and darker stairs, where blue is darkened on blueness.
Even where Persephone goes, just now, from the frosted September
to the sightless realm where darkness is awake upon the dark
and Persephone herself is but a voice
or a darkness invisible enfolded in the deeper dark
of the arms of Plutonic, and pierced with the passion of dense gloom,
among the splendour of torches of darkness, shedding darkness on the lost
bride and her groom.

D. H. Lawrence, 1885-1930

MICHAELMAS DAISIES

T HE early days of October bring with them the best bloom of the Michaelmas Daisies, the many beautiful garden kinds of the perennial Asters. They have, as they well deserve to have, a garden to themselves. Passing along the wide path in front of the big flower border, and through the pergola that forms its continuation, with eye and brain full of rich, warm colouring of flower and leaf, it is a delightful surprise to pass through the pergola's last right-hand opening, and to come suddenly upon the Michaelmas Daisy garden in full beauty. Its clean, fresh, pure colouring, of pale and dark lilac, strong purple, and pure white, among masses of pale-green foliage, forms a contrast almost startling after the warm colouring of nearly everything else; and the sight of a region where the flowers are fresh and newly opened, and in glad spring-like profusion, when all else is on the verge of death and decay, gives an impression of satisfying refreshment that is hardly to be equalled throughout the year.

From *Wood and Garden* by Gertrude Jekyll, 1843-1932

GATHERING LEAVES

SPADES take up leaves
No better than spoons,
And bags full of leaves
Are light as balloons.

I make a great noise
Of rustling all day
Like a rabbit and deer
Running away.

But the mountains I raise
Elude my embrace,
Flowing over my arms
And into my face.

I may load and unload
Again and again
Till I fill the whole shed,
And what have I then?

Next to nothing for weight;
And since they grew duller
From contact with earth,
Next to nothing for color.

Next to nothing for use.
But a crop is a crop,
And who's to say where
The harvest shall stop?

Robert Frost, 1874-1963

FOG

LONDON. Michaelmas Term lately over, and the Lord Chancellor sitting in Lincoln's Inn Hall. Implacable November weather. As much mud in the streets, as if the waters had but newly retired from the face of the earth, and it would not be wonderful to meet a Megalosaurus, forty feet long or so, waddling like an elephantine lizard up Holborn Hill. Smoke lowering down from chimney-pots, making a soft black drizzle, with flakes of soot in it as big as full-grown snow-flakes – gone into mourning, one might imagine, for the death of the sun. Dogs, undistinguishable in mire. Horses, scarcely better; splashed to their very blinkers. Foot passengers, jostling one another's umbrellas, in a general infection of ill temper, and losing their foot-hold at street corners, where tens of thousands of other foot passengers have been slipping and sliding since the day broke (if this day ever broke), adding new deposits to the crust upon crust of mud, sticking at those points tenaciously to the pavement, and accumulating at compound interest.

Fog everywhere. Fog up the river, where it flows among green aits and meadows; fog down the river, where it rolls defiled among the tiers of shipping, and the waterside pollutions of a great (and dirty) city. Fog on the Essex marshes, fog on the Kentish heights. Fog creeping into the cabooses of collier-brigs; fog lying out on the yards, and hovering in the rigging of great ships; fog drooping on the gunwales of barges and small boats. Fog in the eyes and throats of ancient Greenwich pensioners, wheezing by the firesides of their wards; fog in the stem and bowl of the afternoon pipe of the wrathful skipper, down in his close cabin; fog cruelly pinching the toes and fingers of his shivering little 'prentice boy on deck. Chance people on the bridges peeping over the parapets into a nether sky of fog, with fog all round them as if they were up in a balloon, and hanging in the misty clouds.

From *Bleak House* by Charles Dickens, 1812-1870

APPLE HARVEST

OUR Apple harvest has been over for nearly a fortnight; but how pleasant the orchard was while it lasted, and how pleasant the seat in the corner by the Limes, whence we see the distant spire on the green wooded slopes. The grey, gnarled old Apple-trees have, for the most part, done well. The Ribston Pippins are especially fine, and so is an apple, which we believe to be the King of the Pippins. On the other hand, we have some poor and worthless sorts – probably local varieties, – which no pomologist, however able and obliging, would undertake to name. One of the prettiest of Apples – and one of the best, too – is the Delaware. It has an orange-red colour, and reminds one almost of an Orange as it hangs upon the tree. It has a crisp, delicious flavour, but requires to be eaten as soon as it is ripe, for otherwise it soon gets mealy. Indeed all eating apples, with but few exceptions, are best when freshly gathered, or, better still, when, on some clear soft day, they have just fallen on the grass, and lie there, warmed by the rays of the autumn sun.

From *A Year in a Lancashire Garden* by Henry A. Bright, 1891

WENLOCK EDGE

On Wenlock Edge the wood's in trouble;
His forest fleece the Wrekin heaves;
The gale, it plies the saplings double,
And thick on Severn snow the leaves.

'Twould blow like this through holt and hanger
When Uricon the city stood:
'Tis the old wind in the old anger,
But then it threshed another wood.

Then, 'twas before my time, the Roman
At yonder heaving hill would stare:
The blood that warms an English yeoman,
The thoughts that hurt him, they were there.

There, like the wind through woods in riot,
Through him the gale of life blew high;
The tree of man was never quiet:
Then 'twas the Roman, now 'tis I.

The gale, it plies the saplings double,
It blows so hard, 'twill soon be gone:
To-day the Roman and his trouble
Are ashed under Uricon.

A. E. Houseman, 1859-1936

GRONGAR HILL

BELOW me Trees unnumber'd rise,
Beautiful in various Dies:
The gloomy Pine, the Poplar blue,
The yellow Beech, the sable Yew,
The slender Firr, that taper grows,
The sturdy Oak with broad-spread Boughs;
And beyond the purple Grove,
Haunt of *Phillis*, Queen of Love!
Gawdy as the op'ning Dawn,
Lies a long and level Lawn,
On which a dark Hill, steep and high,
Holds and charms the wand'ring Eye!

John Dyer, 1699-1758

OCTOBER

O LOVE, turn from the unchanging sea, and gaze
Down these grey slopes upon the year grown old,
A-dying mid the autumn-scented haze,
That hangeth o'er the hollow in the wold,
Where the wind-bitten ancient elms enfold
Grey church, long barn, orchard, and red-roofed stead,
Wrought in dead days for men a long while dead.

Come down, O love; may not our hands still meet,
Since still we live today, forgetting June,
Forgetting May, deeming October sweet –
– O hearken, hearken! through the afternoon,
The grey tower sings a strange old tinkling tune!
Sweet, sweet, and sad, the toiling year's last breath,
Too satiate of life to strive with death.

And we too – will it not be soft and kind,
That rest from life, from patience and from pain;
That rest from bliss we know not when we find;
That rest from Love which ne'er the end can gain? –
Hark, how the tune swells, that erewhile did wane!
Look up, love! – ah, cling close and never move!
How can I have enough of life and love?

From *The Earthly Paradise* by William Morris, 1834-1896

TO AUTUMN

SEASON of mists and mellow fruitfulness,
    Close bosom-friend fo the maturing sun;
  Conspiring with him how to load and bless
With fruit the vines that round the thatch-eves run;
  To bend with apples the moss'd cottage-trees,
    And fill all fruit with ripeness to the core;
  To swell the gourd, and plump the hazel shells
    With a sweet kernel; to set budding more,
    And still more, later flowers for the bees,
  Until they think warm days will never cease,
For Summer has o'er-brimm'd their clammy cells.

  Who hath not seen thee oft amid thy store?
  Sometimes whoever seeks abroad may find
    Thee sitting careless on a granary floor,
    Thy hair soft-lifted by winnowing wind;
  Or on a half-reap'd furrow sound asleep,
Drows'd with the fume of poppies, while thy hook
  Spares the next swath and all its twined flowers:
    And sometimes like a gleaner thou dost keep
    Steady thy laden head across a brook;
    Or by a cyder-press, with patient look,
  Thou watchest the last oozings hours by hours.

Where are the songs of Spring? Ay, where are they?
  Think not of them, thou hast thy music too, —
  While barred clouds bloom the soft-dying day,
    And touch the stubble-plains with rosy hue;
  Then in a wailful choir the small gnats mourn
    Among the river sallows, borne aloft
    Or sinking as the light wind lives or dies;
And full-grown lambs loud bleat from hilly bourn;
  Hedge-crickets sing; and now with treble soft
    The red-breast whistles from a garden-croft;
  And gathering swallows twitter in the skies.

John Keats, 1795-1821

ACKNOWLEDGEMENTS

Bridgeman Art Library:

p3 *Winter Scene and Figures Skating*: Esaias I Van de Velde/Harold Samuel Collection, Corporation of London; p7 *The Fern Gatherer*: C S Lidderdale/Phillips International Fine Art Auctioneers; p11 *Portrait of Mrs Kathleen Newton*: James Jacques Tissot/ Private Collection; p12 *Man in a Fur Coat*: Robert Oswald Moser/Christopher Wood Gallery, London; p15 *Ode to Music*: John Melhuish Strudwick/Roy Miles Fine Paintings, London; p21 *The Christening* (detail): Edward Bird/Wolverhampton Art Gallery; p22 *Mr Fezziwig's Ball*: John Leech/V&A; p25 *The Trianon Under Snow*: Henri Eugene Augustin Le Sidaner/Private Collection; p26 *The Waltz*: Joseph Marius Avy/Whitford & Hughes, London; p29 *February, Les Tres Riches Heures du Duc de Berry*/V&A; p30 *Home*: Carlton Alfred Smith/Christie's, London; p37 *Winter Days*: George Henry Boughton/Fine Art Society, London; p38 *Snowballing*: Cornelius Kimmel/Gavin Graham Gallery, London; p39 *Advertisement for Christmas Hampers*/ Private Collection; p40/41 *Dinner at the Temple of Prince of Conti*: Michel Barthelemy Olivier/Chateau de Versailles, France; p43 *Christmas Roses*: Willem van Leen/Gavin Graham Gallery, London; p44 *Mlle Croizette*: Charles Emile Auguste Carolus-Duran/ Musée Des Beaux Arts, Touroing; p46 *Franz Schubert at the Piano*: Gustav Klimt/ Archiv Für Kunst und Geschichte, Berlin; p48 *My Second Sermon*: Sir John Everett Millais/Guildhall Art Gallery; p55 *A Woman by a Fireside*: Marcus Stone/Agnew & Sons, London; p59 *The Clifton Assembly Rooms*: Rolinda Sharples/City of Bristol Museum & Art Gallery; p61 *A Day in Late Autumn*: E W Waite/Private Collection; p63 *The Mistletoe Gatherer*: Sir John Everett Millais/Private Collection.

David Messum Galleries, London & Beaconsfield:
p13 *The Evening Shawl*: Archibald Barnes; p18 *The Goldfish Bowl*: Wilfred de Glehn; p33 *Fairy Tales*: George Harcourt.

Fine Art Photographic Archive:
p9 *Carriage to a Ball*: William Bromley; p17 *Madame Se Chauffe*: John Callcott Horsley; p20 *New Year's Eve*: William Henry Boot; p42 *Flowers of Shakespeare*: Anon; p45 *Redwing During Frost*: Archibald Thorburn; p47 *Paris*: Louis Besson; p56/57 *St Paul's from the River*: George Hyde Pownall.

Manya Igel Fine Arts/The Medici Society: p5 *Frozen Out*: George Dunlop Leslie.

National Gallery:
p35 *A Winter Scene with Skaters near a Castle*: Henrick Avercamp.

Richard Hagen Fine Paintings, Worcestershire:
p50 *The Skater* (detail): Edward John Gregory.

Royal Academy of Arts: p52 *Green Park*: Robert Buhler.

Cover: *The Mistletoe Gatherer*: Sir John Everett Millais/Private Collection/ The Bridgeman Art Library.

FOREST'S ROBE

Penhaligon's autumn pot-pourri is called Forest's Robe, composed of the bark, oakmoss, pine cones and other treasures of the forest floor.

Oakmoss is gathered from the old oak forests of Eastern Europe and buckthorn bark comes from the great trees of North America. These are mixed with cypress cones, bay and uva ursi leaves, bakuli nuts from Malasia, alder seed pods and cassurina cones from the Mediterranean.

With its natural blend of wood and moss, Forest's Robe has a beguiling green scent which perfumes the endpapers of this book and perfectly captures the spirit of autumn.

Design by Andrew Barron and Collis Clements Associates
Original design concept by Bernard Higton
Picture research by Lynda Marshall
Jacket background design originated by Flo Bayley for Penhaligon's Limited.

Published in the United States by Harmony Books,
a division of Crown Publishers, Inc.,
201 East 50th Street, New York, New York 10022

First published in Great Britain in 1992 by Pavilion Books Limited

Harmony and Colophon are trademarks of Crown Publishers, Inc.

Manufactured in Singapore by Imago

ISBN 0-517-58939-7

First American Edition

10 9 8 7 6 5 4 3 2 1

If you would like more information on
Penhaligon's Forest's Robe, with which this book is scented,
or any other of the Penhaligon gifts or products,
please telephone London 011-44-81-880-2050, or write to:
PENHALIGON'S
41 Wellington Street, Covent Garden, London WC2